COMMON CORE
LANGUAGE ARTS
GRADE 2

Suzanne Forbes

Lindsay Forbes

Common Core Education, Inc.
1695 Olinda Road
Makawao, Maui, HI 96768
www.CommonCoreEducation.com
ISBN-13: 978-0615514307
ISBN-10: 0615514308
©2011 Common Core Education, Inc.
Printed in the United States of America

Common Core State Standards for English Language Arts © Copyright 2010.
National Governors Association Center for Best Practices and Council of Chief
State School Officers. All rights reserved.

Graphics provided by Microsoft
Cover design by Jessica Matsumoto

TABLE OF CONTENTS

LANGUAGE STANDARD 1: Demonstrate command of the conventions of standard English grammar and usage when writing or speaking.

LANGUAGE STANDARD 2: Demonstrate command of the conventions of standard English capitalization, punctuation, and spelling when writing.

LANGUAGE STANDARD 4: Determine or clarify the meaning of unknown and multiple-meaning words and phrases based on grade 2 reading and content, choosing flexibly from an array of strategies.

LANGUAGE STANDARD 5: Demonstrate understanding of word relationships and nuances in word meanings.

Name _____

Write the correct word from the word box on each blank to complete each phrase.

| school | gaggle | flock | group | herd |

1. one goose in a _____ of geese

2. one cow in a _____ of cows

3. one fish in a _____ of fish

4. one sheep in a _____ of sheep

5. one child in a _____ of children

Use a word from the word box to write your own sentence.

1. _____

_____

L.2.1.a

Name _____

Write the correct word from the word box on each blank to complete each phrase.

| bunch | batch | pack | bouquet |

1. one wolf in a _____ of wolves

2. one grape in a _____ of grapes

3. one flower in a _____ of flowers

4. one cookie in a _____ of cookies

Use two different words from the word box to write your own sentences.

1. _____

_____

2. _____

_____

Name _____

1. I lost a **tooth**. I have lost three _____ altogether.

2. One **child** wants to play with all of the other _____.

3. The little **mouse** was not as big as the other five _____ in the cage.

4. The _____ were running behind their lead **wolf**.

5. That **woman** is taller than the other _____.

6. The **man** invited the other _____ to watch the game.

Name _____

Draw a line to match the singular noun
with its plural form.

1. tooth   wolves

2. woman   feet

3. goose   teeth

4. foot   men

5. child   sheep

6. mouse   mice

7. sheep   women

8. wolf   geese

9. man   children

L.2.1.b

Name _____

Example: Did you loose **a tooth**?
            <u>Did you loose teeth?</u>

1. I saw **a goose** fly over the hill.

    _____

    _____

2. **A mouse** ran under our feet.

    _____

    _____

3. I caught **a fish** when I went fishing!

    _____

    _____

4. The **woman** went into the hardware store.

    _____

    _____

Name _____

1. I saw a flock of (sheep/sheeps) eating some grass.

2. There was a noisy group of (childs/children) in the lunch room.

3. My boots do not fit on my (foots/feet).

4. A school of (fish/fishes) swam in the ocean.

5. The owl watched as the (mice/mouses) ran across the field.

6. I have already lost two baby (teeth/tooths).

7. The (mooses/moose) stamped in the snow.

8. If you scare the (deer/deers) they will run.

9. The (wolfs/wolves) howl at night.

Name _____

1. In the morning, I choose my clothes by (ourselves/myself).

2. Carly can make breakfast by (sheself/herself).

3. Did Manny go by (himself/themselves)?

4. We can dress (ourselves/myself).

5. They played a game by (himself/themselves).

6. Can you lift this box by (himself/yourself)?

7. He walked upstairs by (hisself/himself).

8. My Aunt Carol likes to read by (himself/ herself).

9. Please help (yourself/ourselves) to a cookie.

10. Dana and Chuck went by (theyselves/ themselves).

11. I baked the cake all by (myself/yourself)!

L.2.1.c

Name _____

| myself | yourself | herself | himself |

1. I make my bed by _____.

2. Can you ride a bike by _____?

3. I chose a book for _____.

4. Did he see _____ in the mirror?

5. Make _____ comfortable while you are waiting.

6. My little sister always wants to do things by _____.

7. Mr. Dan wants to buy _____ a new car.

8. Did you plan to do it all by _____?

Name _____

Write sentences that tell what
you can do by yourself.

Example: I can get dressed by myself.

1. _____

   _____

2. _____

   _____

3. _____

   _____

4. _____

   _____

5. _____

   _____

L.2.1.c

Name _____

Finish the sentence to tell what
you are doing in your picture.

I can _____

by myself.

Name _____

1. The farmer (sitted/sat) on a rock to rest.

2. The alarm (rang/ringed) loudly.

3. The deer (hid/hided) behind a tree.

4. Grandma (telled/told) me a story last night.

5. The story (beginned/began) with a handsome prince.

6. The spy (drew/drawed) a map.

7. We (goed/went) to Spain with Grandpa.

8. Nigel and Brian (made/maked) a fort out of sticks.

9. The zebra (ran/runned) across the grass.

10. The puppy (digged/dug) a hole in the yard and (finded/found) a bone.

L.2.1.d

Name _____

1. My kitten (drank/drinked) from its bowl.

2. She (bringed/brought) extra sunscreen.

3. Yesterday my new toy (braked/broke).

4. My father (builded/built) a fort for me in the backyard.

5. My mother (drove/drived) to school to pick me up.

6. When I was sick I (getted/got) to eat ice cream.

7. Nina was sad when she (sold/selled) her old bike.

8. We (standed/stood) in line for a long time.

9. My brother (teached/taught) me how to play basketball.

Name _____

Example: Today I give my homework to the her.
           Yesterday I <u>gave my homework to her.</u>

1. Today I **go** to swim practice.

Yesterday I _____

_____.

2. Today Marcy **makes** yummy jam.

Yesterday Marcy _____

_____.

3. Today the owl **flies** over the trees.

Yesterday the owl _____

_____.

4. Today Joey **rides** the bus to school.

Yesterday Joey _____

_____.

L.2.1.d

Name _____

Complete each sentence using the past tense.

Example: Today I make pies.
             Yesterday I <u>made pies.</u>

1.   Today I **buy** chocolate donuts.

Yesterday I _____

_____.

2.   Today Pat **brings** his lunch to school.

Yesterday Pat _____

_____.

3.   Today Dad **sells** his old car.

Yesterday Dad _____

_____.

4.   Today Ms. Vila **teaches** math.

Yesterday Ms. Vila _____

_____.

Name _____

Example: Yesterday Mom drove to work.
Today Mom <u>drives to work</u>.

1. Yesterday I **went** to his house after school.

Today I _____

_____.

2. Yesterday Eric **held** the flag.

Today Eric _____

_____.

3. Yesterday Betty **brought** apples to school.

Today Betty _____

_____.

4. Yesterday Grandpa **began** reading to me.

Today Grandpa _____

_____

_____.

Name _____

Example: Yesterday Kim swam in the pool.
                   Today Kim <u>swims in the pool</u>.

1.   Yesterday we **hid** the present in the closet.

Today we _____

_____.

2.   Yesterday Kimo **drew** a picture of the ocean.

Today Kimo _____

_____.

3.   Yesterday Tom **got** to lead the class.

Today Tom _____

_____.

4.   Yesterday Nana **rang** the dinner bell.

Today Nana _____

_____.

Name _____

1. The train is moving (quick/quickly).

2. The train is (quick/quickly).

3. The porch light is (bright/brightly).

4. The porch light shines (bright/brightly).

5. The drum is (loud/loudly).

6. The drum beats (loud/loudly).

7. The turtle moves (slow/slowly).

8. The turtle is (slow/slowly).

9. The dog is (noisy/noisily).

10. The dog barks (noisy/noisily).

11. The child is (happy/happily).

12. The child plays (happy/happily).

13. Is the boy (sad/sadly)?

14. The boy is (sad/sadly).

15. The boy walks (sad/sadly).

L.2.1.e

Name _____

1. The (quick/quickly) rabbit got away.

2. The rabbit (quick/quickly) hid behind the tree.

3. The rabbit is (quick/quickly).

4. The rabbit ran (quick/quickly).

5. The (loud/loudly) horn scared my little sister.

6. The horn (loud/loudly) blared for an hour.

7. The horn is (loud/loudly).

8. The horn blared (loud/loudly).

9. The (happy/happily) baby played with toys.

10. The baby (happy/happily) played.

11. The baby is (happy/happily).

12. The baby played (happy/happily).

Name _____

| quietly | loudly | happy | playfully | muddy |

Paco's Bath

"It's time for a bath, Paco!" shouted Joan to her little dog. Paco had been playing in the _____ yard. His fur was very dirty.

Paco did not want to get a bath. Joan had to talk _____ to Paco to keep him calm while she carried him to the bathroom.

Joan put Paco in the bathtub, and he barked _____. He was not _____.

As Joan washed Paco, he calmed down and licked Joan's cheek. It was Paco's way of saying, "Thank you!"

Joan dried Paco's fur with a towel. Paco _____ grabbed the towel and ran away.

Paco's bath is always an adventure!

L.2.1.e   ©2011 Common Core Education, Inc.

Name _____

| silly | quickly | large | tightly | gently |

How to Build a Snowman

First, make three small, round snowballs. Pack them _____ so they don't fall apart.

Next, roll each snowball through the snow to make three body parts. You will need to make one small, one medium, and one _____ ball.

After you finish making the body parts, stack one on top of the other. _____ pack more snow where the parts connect. Be careful!

Now you can decorate your snowman. Use rocks to make eyes, sticks to make arms, and a big carrot for the nose. Remember to add a _____ hat, too!

The sun will _____ melt your snowman, so enjoy him while you can!

Name _____

Example: George is sick.
            <u>Poor George is sick with a terrible flu</u>.

1. The boy watched the movie.

    _____

    _____

2. The boat went under the bridge.

    _____

    _____

3. The zebra ran.

    _____

    _____

Name _____

Example: The chicken ate.
           The white chicken quickly ate corn.

1. I like to read.

   _____

   _____

2. The circus is fun.

   _____

   _____

3. The monkey danced.

   _____

   _____

   _____

Name _____

Expand each sentence.

Example: The whale swam in the ocean.
<u>The gentle whale swam gracefully in the deep blue ocean.</u>

1. The pig rolled in the mud.

   _____

   _____

   _____

2. A butterfly landed on a flower.

   _____

   _____

   _____

3. The truck honked its horn.

   _____

   _____

   _____

Name _____

Expand each sentence.

Example: The baby laughed.
<u>The cute and chubby baby laughed joyfully when he saw the puppy.</u>

1. The rabbit hopped.

    _____

    _____

    _____

2. A cow slept in the field.

    _____

    _____

    _____

3. The bird sang.

    _____

    _____

    _____

Name _____

1. christmas and hanukkah are winter holidays.

2. muslims celebrate a month called ramadan.

3. you may get a special card on valentine's day!

4. People wear costumes on the jewish holiday purim.

5. in april, we plant trees for earth day.

6. in america, many people celebrate thanksgiving each november.

7. january 1 is new year's day around the world.

8. beware of tricks on april fool's day!

9. ratha yatra is a hindu festival.

10. do you dress up for halloween?

L.2.2.a

Name _____

Rewrite the sentences using capital letters when necessary.

1. the country china is located in asia.

_____

_____

2. last summer i visited spain and italy in europe.

_____

_____

3. the eiffel tower is located in france.

_____

_____

4. i'll bet it is really cold in antarctica!

_____

_____

Name _____

1. most people in south america speak spanish.

   _____

   _____

2. jordan visited the great wall of china in may.

   _____

   _____

3. can we visit the grand canyon in arizona?

   _____

   _____

4. the statue of liberty is near ellis island.

   _____

   _____

Name _____

1. cinderella castle is located at walt disney world in florida.

2. disneyland in california is home to sleeping beauty castle.

3. if you visit the parks in october, you may see halloween decorations.

4. as you walk down main street, usa, you may see mary poppins or alice in wonderland.

5. sometimes buzz lightyear waves to visitors near space mountain in tomorrowland.

6. if you see captain hook, look for peter pan and tinkerbell.

7. if you are lucky, you will see mickey mouse and minnie mouse in the parade.

8. mr. walt disney had a wonderful imagination!

*All locations and characters on this page are property of the Walt Disney Company.

Name _____

May 24 1974

Dear Janet

How are you? I heard that you are visiting China in the spring. I want to visit someday.

Sincerely

Beth

June 22 1974

Dear Beth

I am fine and hope you are, too. I am really looking forward to my visit to China. I will send a postcard to you!

Sincerely

Janet

L.2.2.b

Insert commas where necessary.

September 3 2001

Dear Howard

　　Happy birthday! I hope you enjoy your day and get lots of presents. I am looking forward to your party on Saturday afternoon.

　　　　　　　Love

　　　　　　　Sue

September 15 2001

Dear Sue

　　Thank you for coming to my birthday party! I hope you had fun. Thank you also for my present. I hope to see you again soon.

　　　　　　　Love

　　　　　　　Howard

　　　L.2.2.b

Name _____

August 10 2005

Dear Chaz

How is summer camp? Are you doing anything fun? I miss you and can't wait to see you when you get back next month.

Your friend

Derek

August 12 2005

Dear Derek

Summer camp is fun. I got to row a boat on the lake. I also got to jump off the high diving board. I was really scared, but I did it!

Your friend

Chaz

Name _____

Insert commas where necessary.

August 15 2005

Dear Chaz

    Thank you for writing back to me. It sounds like you are having a good time at summer camp. When you get home I want to hear more about it.

          Your friend

          Derek

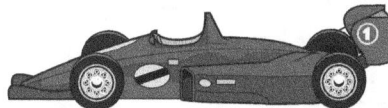

August 20 2005

Dear Derek

    When I get back I will show you the pictures I have been taking with my new camera. I also want to show you the model race car I built.

          Your friend

          Chaz

Name _____

Rewrite the letter on the lines below. Remember to use commas and capitals where necessary.

july 9 2011

dear aunt liza

    thank you letting me visit you in hawaii. i had a really good time at baldwin beach and iao valley. it was fun to see the fireworks on independence day, too.

        love
        zyler

_____

_____

_____

_____

_____

_____

_____

_____

L.2.2.a/L.2.2.b

Name _____

---

april 1 1997

dear yoshi

    last night a big green alien wearing white gloves visited me. he ate all of my puffy pops cereal. then he left without saying goodbye. happy april fool's day!

        your friend
        brandon

                    _____

_____

    _____

_____

_____

_____

   _____

                    _____

Name _____

Example: did not   <u>didn't</u>

1. he will   _____

2. she will   _____

3. we will   _____

4. they will   _____

5. I will   _____

6. will not   _____

7. did not   _____

8. cannot   _____

9. should not   _____

10. would not   _____

Write a sentence that has at least one contraction.

_____

_____

_____

L.2.2.c

Name _____

Example: will not   <u>won't</u>

1. I have   _____

2. you have   _____

3. we have   _____

4. they have   _____

5. I would   _____

6. you would   _____

7. we would   _____

8. they would   _____

9. he would   _____

10. she would   _____

Write a sentence that has at least one contraction.

_____

_____

_____

Name _____

Example: did not   <u>didn't</u>

1. is not   _____

2. has not   _____

3. will not   _____

4. they are   _____

5. you are   _____

6. we are   _____

7. he is   _____

8. she is   _____

9. he had   _____

10. she had   _____

Write a sentence that has at least one contraction.

_____

_____

_____

L.2.2.c

Name _____

Underline the correct spelling of the contraction in each sentence.

1. I (can't/ca'nt) wait for summer!

2. You (don't/do'nt) like grape juice.

3. My mother (willn't/won't) let me eat sweets.

4. (Iv'e/I've) finished all of my homework.

5. She said (she'll/shell) bring it to tomorrow.

6. You (should've/should've) listened to me!

7. Do you think (hel'l/he'll) show up?

8. (He'd/He'ed) like to go with us.

9. (Your/You're) a really good friend.

10. I thought (you'd/you'ld) like it.

11. It looks like (they've/theyv'e) got a lot of work to do on that house.

12. (They're/There) putting on the roof next.

Name _____

Example:

One **boy** has a hat.   It is the <u>boy's</u> hat.

Two **boys** have a hat.   It is the <u>boys'</u> hat.

1.   One **rabbit** has a carrot.

It is the _____ carrot.

Two **rabbits** have a carrot.

It is the _____ carrot.

2.   One **kitten** has a ball of string.

It is the _____ ball of string.

Two **kittens** have a ball of string.

It is the _____ ball of string.

3.   One **brother** has a box of cereal.

It is the _____ box of cereal.

Two **brothers** have a box of cereal.

It is the _____ box of cereal.

Name _____

Write the correct possessive noun on the blank.

Example:
One **girl** has a book.   It is the <u>girl's</u> book.
Two **girls** have a book.   It is the <u>girls'</u> book.

1. One **clown** has a horn.

    It is the _____ horn.

    Two **clowns** have a horn.

    It is the _____ horn.

2. One **chick** has a mama hen.

    It is the _____ mama hen.

    Two **chicks** have a mama hen.

    It is the _____ mama hen.

3. One **sister** has a brother.

    It is the _____ brother.

    Two **sisters** have a brother.

    It is the _____ brother.

L.2.2.c

Name _____

Example: Those toys belong to the kids.
Those are the <u>kids'</u> toys.

1. The rakes belong to the farmers.

    Those are the _____ rakes.

2. The wheels belong to the trucks.

    Those are the _____ wheels.

3. The stripes belong to the zebras.

    Those are the _____ stripes.

4. The sails belong to the ships.

    Those are the _____ sails.

5. The shoes belong to the men.

    Those are the _____ shoes.

6. The bananas belong to the monkeys.

    Those are the _____ bananas.

L.2.2.c

Name _____

| Write the correct possessive noun on the blank. |

Example: Those hats belong to the ladies.
           Those are the <u>ladies'</u> hats.

1. The scales belong to the snakes.

    Those are the _____ scales.

2. The carts belong to the stores.

    Those are the _____ carts.

3. The picnic tables belong to the parks.

    Those are the _____ picnic

    tables.

4. The nests belong to the robins.

    Those are the _____ nests.

5. The games belong to the children.

    Those are the _____ games.

6. The petals belong to the flowers.

    Those are the _____ petals.

Name _____

1. A (tiger's/tigers') fur is orange and black.

2. The (policeman's/policemans') badge is shiny.

3. The (children's/childrens') books are in their bags.

4. The three (kitten's/kittens') noses were wet.

5. The four (boat's/boats') sails puffed with wind.

6. A (storm's/storms') clouds are dark and gray.

7. The two (game's/games') pieces are on the floor!

8. The (sand's/sands') grains are very tiny.

9. One (dog's/dogs') collar was blue.

10. Where is the (men's/mens') room located?

11. The second grade (teacher's/teachers') classrooms are in this building.

L.2.2.c

Name _____

Underline the correct possessive noun
in each sentence.

1. Please put the (milk's/milks') cap back on.

2. My (computer's/computers') screen is dusty.

3. The (egg's/eggs') carton keeps them from breaking.

4. The four (pillow's/pillows') covers matched the sofa.

5. The (broom's/brooms') handle broke.

6. How may legs are on one (ant's/ants) body?

7. My (book's/books') covers are red, blue, and green.

8. The (chimney's/chimneys') opening let the smoke out.

9. The (car's/cars') engines roared before the start of the race.

10. The (piglet's/piglets') noses were pink.

Name _____

Use the context clues in the sentence to determine the meaning of the underlined word.

1. The squirrels, rabbits, and skunks lived deep in the wilderness and away from the humans.

   Circle the word that has almost the same meaning as the word wilderness:

   city   woods   playground

2. When the fire alarm began ringing, we immediately lined up at the door.

   Circle the word that has almost the same meaning as the word immediately.

   slowly   quickly   later

3. The new student was quiet and bashful when the teacher introduced him to the class.

   Circle the word that has almost the same meaning as the word bashful.

   shy   loud   lazy

L.2.4.a

Name _____

Use the context clues in the sentence to determine the meaning of the underlined word.

1. Miguel held the scared baby bird <u>tenderly</u> in his hand.

   Circle the word that has almost the same meaning as the word <u>tenderly</u>:

   tightly   gently   loudly

2. The pirates got excited when they saw the <u>gleaming</u> jewels and coins.

   Circle the word that has almost the same meaning as the word <u>gleaming</u>.

   shining   dirty   square

3. The <u>pathetic</u> lost puppy stared at Jonelle with its big eyes, so she took it home.

   Circle the word that has almost the same meaning as the word <u>pathetic</u>.

   sparkling   gigantic   sad

Name _____

1. The group asked us to <u>donate</u> used toys and clothing to the people who lost everything.

   Circle the word that has almost the same meaning as the word <u>donate</u>:

   paint   build   give

2. My brother and I often <u>quarrel</u> about whose turn it is to do the dishes.

   Circle the word that has almost the same meaning as the word <u>quarrel</u>.

   sing   argue   write

3. The guests had a <u>splendid</u> time at the beach party.

   Circle the word that has almost the same meaning as the word <u>splendid</u>.

   sandy   wet   wonderful

Name _____

1. The man was <u>parched</u> after walking three days in the desert with nothing to drink.

    Circle the word that has almost the same meaning as the word <u>parched</u>:

    hungry   thirsty   surprised

2. My dog goes <u>berserk</u> when a stranger rings our doorbell.

    Circle the word or phrase that has almost the same meaning as the word <u>berserk</u>.

    quiet   tame   crazy

3. The <u>elderly</u> man and woman were excited to see their grandchildren.

    Circle the word that has almost the same meaning as the word <u>elderly.</u>

    strange   old   young

Name _____

Add the prefix **un–** to each word and write the new word on the blank. Then write the meaning of the new word.

Example: un + lucky = <u>unlucky</u>
            and that means <u>not lucky</u>

1. un + happy = _____

    and that means _____

2. un + able = _____

    and that means _____

3. un + afraid = _____

    and that means _____

4. un + broken = _____

    and that means _____

5. un + clean = _____

    and that means _____

6. un + equal = _____

    and that means _____

L.2.4.b

Name _____

Add the prefix **un–** to each word and write the new word on the blank. Then write the meaning of the new word.

Example: un + happy = <u>unhappy</u>
           and that means <u>not happy</u>

1. un + even =   _____

    and that means _____

2. un + fair =   _____

    and that means _____

3. un + healthy = _____

    and that means _____

4. un + kind =   _____

    and that means _____

5. un + lit =   _____

    and that means _____

6. un + lucky =   _____

    and that means _____

L.2.4.b   50

Name _____

Add the prefix **un–** to each adjective (describing word) and write the new word on the blank. Then write the meaning of the new word.

Example: un + able = <u>unable</u>
                    and that means <u>not able</u>

1. un + important = _____

    and that means _____

2. un + salted =   _____

    and that means _____

3. un + ready =   _____

    and that means _____

4. un + real =   _____

    and that means _____

5. un + ripe =   _____

    and that means _____

6. un + safe =   _____

    and that means _____

L.2.4.b

Name _____

Add the prefix **un–** to each adjective (describing word) and write the new word on the blank. Then write the meaning of the new word.

Example: un + wash = <u>unwashed</u>
             and that means <u>not washed</u>

1. un + used =   _____

    and that means _____

2. un + sure =   _____

    and that means _____

3. un + sweetened = _____

    and that means _____

4. un + true =   _____

    and that means _____

5. un + quiet =   _____

    and that means _____

6. un + welcome =   _____

    and that means _____

Name _____

Add the prefix **un–** to each verb (action word) and write the new word on the blank. Then write the meaning of the new word.

Example: un + tie = <u>tie</u>
             and that means <u>undo the tie</u>

1.   un + fold = _____

     and that means _____

2.   un + cover =   _____

     and that means _____

3.   un + lock =   _____

     and that means _____

4.   un + wrap =   _____

     and that means _____

5.   un + roll =   _____

     and that means _____

6.   un + plug =   _____

     and that means _____

L.2.4.b

Name _____

Add the prefix **un–** to each verb (action word) and write the new word on the blank. Then write the meaning of the new word.

Example: un + fold = <u>unfold</u>
             and that means <u>undo the fold</u>

1.   un + zip =   _____

and that means _____

2.   un + curl = _____

and that means _____

3.   un + pack =   _____

and that means _____

4.   un + do =   _____

and that means _____

5.   un + stick =   _____

and that means _____

6.   un + glue =   _____

and that means _____

Name _____

Add the prefix **re–** to each adjective (describing word) and write the new word on the blank. Then write the meaning of the new word.

Example: re + send = <u>resend</u>
          and that means <u>send again</u>

1. re + create = _____

    and that means _____

2. re + state = _____

    and that means _____

3. re + appear = _____

    and that means _____

4. re + build = _____

    and that means _____

5. re + charge = _____

    and that means _____

6. re + write = _____

    and that means _____

L.2.4.b

Name _____

Add the prefix **re–** to each adjective (describing word) and write the new word on the blank. Then write the meaning of the new word.

Example: re + charge = <u>recharge</u>
and that means <u>charge again</u>

1.   re + use =   _____

and that means _____

2.   re + do =   _____

and that means _____

3.   re + view =   _____

and that means _____

4.   re + start = _____

and that means _____

5.   re + make =   _____

and that means _____

6.   re + open =   _____

and that means _____

Name _____

Add the prefix **re–** to each verb (action word) and write the new word on the blank. Then write the meaning of the new word.

Example: re + send = <u>resend</u>
                and that means <u>send again</u>

1.   re + pay = _____

     and that means _____

2.   re + new = _____

     and that means _____

3.   re + work =   _____

     and that means _____

4.   re + try =   _____

     and that means _____

5.   re + learn =   _____

     and that means _____

6.   re + teach =   _____

     and that means _____

L.2.4.b

Name _____

Add the prefix **re–** to each verb (action word) and write the new word on the blank. Then write the meaning of the new word.

Example: re + pay = <u>repay</u>
                      and that means <u>pay again</u>

1.   re + run = _____

     and that means _____

2.   re + check = _____

     and that means _____

3.   re + place = _____

     and that means _____

4.   re + set = _____

     and that means _____

5.   re + dress = _____

     and that means _____

6.   re + order = _____

     and that means _____

Name _____

Add the prefix **super–** to each word and write the
new word on the blank. Then write the meaning of
the new word.

Example: super + man = <u>superman</u>
           and that means <u>greater than a man</u>

1.   super + charge = _____

     and that means _____

2.   super + woman = _____

     and that means _____

3.   super + human = _____

     and that means _____

4.   super + star = _____

     and that means _____

5.   super + market = _____

     and that means _____

6.   super + fine = _____

     and that means _____

Name _____

Add the prefix **over–** to each word and write the new word on the blank. Then write the meaning of the new word.

Example: over + pay = <u>overpay</u>
            and that means <u>pay too much</u>

1.   over + do = _____

     and that means _____

2.   over + buy = _____

     and that means _____

3.   over + dress = _____

     and that means _____

4.   over + fill = _____

     and that means _____

5.   over + use = _____

     and that means _____

6.   over + sleep = _____

     and that means _____

L.2.4.b

Name _____

Example: un<u>lock</u>

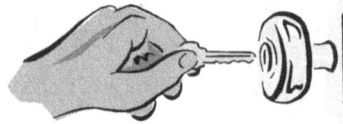

1. sleeping
2. addition
3. older
4. unclean
5. thoughtful
6. undo
7. preview
8. knowledge
9. biggest
10. smaller
11. unhealthy
12. reuse
13. keeping
14. rethink
15. sweeten

16. unhelpful
17. unafraid
18. hopeful
19. pretest
20. review
21. redo
22. alarming
23. friendliness
24. neighborhood
25. unreasonable
26. presale
27. prepay
28. unequal
29. joyful
30. asleep

Name _____

Underline the same root in each group of words.

Example:
    <u>addi</u>tion   <u>addi</u>tional   <u>add</u>ing

1. sleeping   sleeper   asleep

2. unreal   reality   realize

3. overlook   looking   looker

4. infield   outfield   midfield

5. childlike   grandchild   children

6. quietly   quietness   quieter

7. runner   overrun   rerun

8. friendliness   unfriendly   befriend

9. afloat   floating   floater

10. react   actor   interact

11. postscript   prescription   scripture

12. overview   review   preview

13. sadness   sadly   sadden

14. working   rework   worked

15. unknown   knowledge   knowing

Name _____

Example: a birdhouse is <u>a house for birds</u>

1. earphones are _____

    _____

2. firewood is _____

    _____

3. a fishhook is _____

    _____

4. a classroom is _____

    _____

5. moonlight is _____

    _____

6. popcorn is _____

    _____

7. a sailboat is _____

    _____

L.2.4.d

Name _____

Example: moonlight is <u>light from the moon</u>

1.   a washcloth is _____

_____

2.   seafood is _____

_____

3.   a snowman is _____

_____

4.   bedtime is _____

_____

5.   a daydream is _____

_____

6.   a fingernail is _____

_____

7.   a bookcase is _____

_____

Name _____

1. _____

2. _____

3. _____

4. _____

5. _____

6. _____

7. _____

Write a list of **spicy foods.**

1. _____

2. _____

3. _____

4. _____

5. _____

6. _____

7. _____

L.2.5.a

Name _____

Write a list of **useful items.**

1. _____
2. _____
3. _____
4. _____
5. _____
6. _____
7. _____

Write a list of **luxury items.**

1. _____
2. _____
3. _____
4. _____
5. _____
6. _____
7. _____

L.2.5.a

Name _____

Write a list of **sticky foods**.

1. _____

2. _____

3. _____

4. _____

5. _____

6. _____

7. _____

Write a list of **condiments**.

1. _____

2. _____

3. _____

4. _____

5. _____

6. _____

7. _____

L.2.5.a

Name _____

Write a list of **household items.**

1. _____
2. _____
3. _____
4. _____
5. _____
6. _____
7. _____

Write a list of **community workers.**

1. _____
2. _____
3. _____
4. _____
5. _____
6. _____
7. _____

Name _____

Example: big   large   ~~small~~   huge

1.   fast   speedy   slow   swift
2.   throw   step   hurl   toss
3.   thin   skinny   slender   wide
4.   spicy   bland   mild   tasteless
5.   chilly   frigid   warm   cold
6.   massive   tiny   huge   gigantic
7.   petite   enormous   tiny   puny
8.   silent   quiet   loud   soundless
9.   smooth   rough   bumpy   uneven
10. yummy   modern   tasty   delicious

L.2.5.b   ©2011 Common Core Education, Inc.

Name _____

Cross out the word in each group that does not have a similar meaning.

Example: fast   speedy   ~~slow~~   swift

1.   tall   rapid   quick   fast
2.   caring   kind   angry   gentle
3.   pretty   attractive   homely   handsome
4.   dull   sparkly   shiny   shimmery
5.   fantastic   boring   superb   incredible
6.   field   meadow   pasture   lake
7.   burning   smoking   freezing   hot
8.   drizzling   raining   sunny   pouring
9.   sit   tread   stroll   stride
10. bellow   shout   whisper   scream

L.2.5.b

Name _____

Choose the best word for each sentence. Write the word on the blank to complete the sentence.

tossed	hurled

1. The pitcher _____ the ball to the catcher.

   My sister _____ the pillow to my mother.

carry	lug

2. Mr. Lum asked us to _____ our own lunches during the field trip.

   Dad had to _____ all of the heavy suitcases upstairs.

freezing	cold

3. It was starting to get _____, so I put on a sweatshirt.

   It was _____ outside, so we had to put on our hats and winter coats.

Name _____

Choose the best word for each sentence. Write the word on the blank to complete the sentence.

| closed   slammed |

1. Dad _____ the door once everyone was inside.

My little brother _____ the door went he got upset.

| happy   overjoyed |

2. Aunt Jill felt _____ when she won the competition.

Uncle Gary felt _____ when he finally finished his work.

| mad   furious |

3. My mother was _____ when we played ball in the house and broke a vase.

My sister gets _____ when I beat her at checkers.

Name _____

big   gigantic

1. The _____ truck roared down the

highway.

The _____ building almost

touched the clouds.

small   tiny

2. Dana asked for a _____

helping of potatoes.

The bug was so _____ I could

barely see it.

whisper   speak

3. Please _____ clearly so the class

can hear you.

Please _____ so you don't wake

up the baby.

L.2.5.b

Name _____

| slender   scrawny |

1. The lost dog did not eat for three days and became very _____.

    The actress did not eat dessert because she wanted to remain _____.

| glanced   stared |

2. Nico _____ at the bird when it flew over the soccer field.

    Tara _____ at the television when it was time to announce the winner.

| breezy   gusty |

3. Branches fell down from the trees and the power went out on that _____ day.

    Leaves blew across the grassy meadow on that _____ day.

ANSWER KEY

Page 1
1. gander
2. herd
3. school
4. flock
5. group

Page 2
1. pack
2. bunch
3. bouquet
4. batch

Page 3
1. teeth
2. children
3. mice
4. wolves
5. women
6. men

Page 4
1. tooth—teeth
2. woman—women
3. goose—geese
4. foot—feet
5. child—children
6. mouse—mice
7. sheep—sheep
8. wolf—wolves
9. man—men

Page 5
1. I saw geese fly over the hill.
2. Mice ran under our feet.
3. I caught fish when I went fishing!
4. The women went into the hardware store.

Page 6
1. sheep
2. children
3. feet
4. fish
5. mice
6. teeth
7. moose
8. deer
9. wolves

Page 7
1. myself
2. herself
3. himself
4. ourselves
5. themselves
6. yourself
7. himself
8. herself
9. yourself
10. themselves
11. myself

Page 8
1. myself
2. yourself
3. myself
4. himself
5. yourself
6. herself
7. himself
8. yourself

Page 9
(Answers will vary.)

Page 10
(Answers will vary.)

Page 11
1. sat
2. rang
3. hid
4. told
5. began
6. drew
7. went
8. made
9. ran
10. dug, found

75

Page 12
1. drank
2. brought
3. broke
4. built
5. drove
6. got
7. sold
8. stood
9. taught

Page 13
1. Yesterday I went to swim practice.
2. Yesterday Marcy made yummy jam.
3. Yesterday the owl flew over the trees.
4. Yesterday Joey rode the bus to school.

Page 14
1. Yesterday I bought chocolate donuts.
2. Yesterday Pat brought his lunch to school.
3. Yesterday Dad sold his old car.
4. Yesterday Ms. Vila taught math.

Page 15
1. Today I go to his house after school.
2. Today Eric holds the flag.
3. Today Betty brings apples to school.
4. Today Grandpa begins reading to me.

Page 16
1. Today we hide the present in the closet.
2. Today Kimo draws a picture of the ocean.
3. Today Tom gets to lead the class.
4. Today Nana rings the dinner bell.

Page 17
1. quickly
2. quick
3. bright
4. brightly
5. loud
6. loudly
7. slowly
8. slow
9. noisy
10. noisily
11. happy
12. happily
13. sad
14. sad
15. sadly

Page 18
1. quick
2. quickly
3. quick
4. quickly
5. loud
6. loudly
7. loud
8. loudly
9. happy
10. happily
11. happy
12. happily

Page 19
muddy
quietly
loudly
happy
playfully

Page 20
tightly
large
Gently
silly
quickly

Page 21
(Answers will vary.)

Page 22

(Answers will vary.)

Page 23

(Answers will vary.)

Page 24

(Answers will vary.)

Page 25
1. Christmas, Hanukkah
2. Muslims, Ramadan
3. You, Valentine's Day
4. Jewish, Purim
5. In, April, Earth Day
6. In, America, Thanksgiving, November
7. January, New Year's Day
8. Beware, April Fool's Day
9. Ratha Yatra, Hindu
10. Do, Halloween

Page 26
1. The country China is located in Asia.
2. Last summer I visited Spain and Italy in Europe.
3. The Eiffel Tower is located in France.
4. I'll bet it is really cold in Antarctica!

Page 27
1. Most people in South America speak Spanish.
2. Jordan visited the Great Wall of China.
3. Can we visit the Grand Canyon in Arizona?
4. The Statue of Liberty is near Ellis Island.

Page 28
1. Cinderella Castle is located at Walt Disney World in Florida.
2. Disneyland in California is home to Sleeping Beauty Castle.
3. If you visit the parks in October, you may see Halloween decorations.

4. As you walk down Main Street, USA, you may see Mary Poppins or Alice in Wonderland.
5. Sometimes Buzz Lightyear waves to visitors near Space Mountain in Tomorrowland.
6. If you see Captain Hook, look for Peter Pan and Tinkerbell.
7. If you are lucky, you will see Mickey Mouse and Minnie Mouse in the parade.
8. Mr. Walt Disney had a wonderful imagination!

Page 29
May 24, 1974
Dear Janet,
Sincerely,
Beth

June 22, 1974
Dear Beth,
Sincerely,
Janet

Page 30
September 3, 2001
Dear Howard,
Love,
Sue

September 15, 2001
Dear Sue,
Love,
Howard

Page 31
August 10, 2005
Dear Chaz,
Your friend,
Derek

August 12, 2005
Dear Derek,
Your friend,
Chaz

Page 32
August 15, 2005
Dear Chaz,
Your friend,
Derek

August 20, 2005
Dear Derek,
Your friend,
Chaz

Page 33
July 9, 2011
Dear Aunt Liza,
Thank you for letting me visit you in Hawaii. I had a really good time at Baldwin Beach and Iao Valley. It was fun to see the fireworks on Independence Day, too.
Love,
Zyler

Page 34
April 1, 1997
Dear Yoshi,
Last night a big green alien wearing white gloves visited me. He ate all of my Puffy Pops cereal. Then he left without saying goodbye. Happy April Fool's Day!
Your friend,
Brandon

Page 35
1. he'll
2. she'll
3. we'll
4. they'll
5. I'll
6. won't
7. didn't
8. can't
9. shouldn't
10. wouldn't
(Sentences will vary.)

Page 36
1. I've
2. you've
3. we've
4. they've
5. I'd
6. you'd
7. we'd
8. they'd
9. he'd
10. she'd
(Sentences will vary.)

Page 37
1. isn't
2. hasn't
3. won't
4. they're
5. you're
6. we're
7. he's
8. she's
9. he'd
10. she'd
(Sentences will vary.)

Page 38
1. can't
2. don't
3. won't
4. I've
5. she'll
6. should've
7. he'll
8. He'd
9. You're
10. you'd
11. they've
12. They're

Page 39
1. rabbit's, rabbits'
2. kitten's, kittens'
3. brother's, brothers'

Page 40
1. clown's, clowns'
2. chick's, chicks'
3. sister's, sisters'

78

Page 41
1. farmers'
2. trucks'
3. zebras'
4. ships'
5. men's
6. monkeys'

Page 42
1. snakes'
2. stores'
3. parks'
4. robins'
5. children's
6. flowers'

Page 43
1. tiger's
2. policeman's
3. children's
4. kittens'
5. boats'
6. storm's
7. games'
8. sand's
9. dog's
10. men's
11. teachers'

Page 44
1. milk's
2. computer's
3. eggs'
4. pillows'
5. broom's
6. ant's
7. books'
8. chimney's
9. cars'
10. piglets'

Page 45
1. woods
2. quickly
3. shy

Page 46
1. gently
2. shining
3. sad

Page 47
1. give
2. argue
3. wonderful

Page 48
1. thirsty
2. crazy
3. old

Page 49
1. unhappy; not happy
2. unable; not able
3. unafraid; not afraid
4. unbroken; not broken
5. unclean; not clean
6. unequal; not equal

Page 50
1. uneven; not even
2. unfair; not fair
3. unhealthy; not healthy
4. unkind; not kind
5. unlit; not lit
6. unlucky; not lucky

Page 51
1. unimportant; not important
2. unsalted; not salted
3. unread; not ready
4. unreal; not real
5. unripe; not ripe
6. unsafe; not safe

Page 52
1. unused; not used
2. unsure; not sure
3. unsweetened; not sweetened
4. untrue; not true
5. unquiet; not quiet
6. unwelcome; not welcome

Page 53
1. unfold; undo the fold
2. uncover; undo the cover
3. unlock; undo the lock
4. unwrap; undo the wrap
5. unroll; undo the roll
6. unplug; undo the plug

Page 54

1. unzip; undo the zip
2. uncurl; undo the curl
3. unpack; undo the packing
4. undo; undo the doing
5. unstick; undo the sticking
6. unglue; undo the gluing

Page 55

1. recreate; create again
2. restate; state again
3. reappear; appear again
4. rebuild; build again
5. recharge; charge again
6. rewrite; write again

Page 56

1. reuse; use again
2. redo; do again
3. review; view again
4. restart; start again
5. remake; make again
6. reopen; open again

Page 57

1. repay; pay again
2. renew; make new again
3. rework; work again
4. retry; try again
5. relearn; learn again
6. reteach; teach again

Page 58

1. rerun; run again
2. recheck; check again
3. replace; place again
4. reset; set again
5. redress; dress again
6. reorder; order again

Page 59

1. supercharge; greater than a charge
2. superwoman; greater than a woman
3. superhuman; greater than a human
4. superstar; greater than a star
5. supermarket; greater than a market
6. superfine; greater than fine

Page 60

1. overdo; do too much
2. overbuy; buy too much
3. overdress; dress too much
4. overfill; fill too much
5. overuse; use too much
6. oversleep; sleep too much

Page 61

1. sleep
2. add
3. old
4. clean
5. thought
6. do
7. view
8. know
9. big
10. small
11. health
12. use
13. keep
14. think
15. sweet

Page 62

1. sleep
2. real
3. look
4. field
5. child
6. quiet
7. run
8. friend
9. float
10. act
11. script
12. view
13. sad
14. work
15. know

Page 63

1. phones for ears
2. wood for a fire
3. a hook for a fish
4. a room for a class
5. light from the moon
6. corn that pops
7. a boat that sails

Page 64

1. a cloth used for washing
2. food from the sea
3. a man made of snow
4. time for bed
5. a dream during the day
6. a nail on a finger
7. a case for books

Page 65

(Answers will vary.)

Page 66

(Answers will vary.)

Page 67

(Answers will vary.)

Page 68

(Answers will vary.)

Page 69

1. slow
2. step
3. wide
4. spicy
5. warm
6. tiny
7. enormous
8. loud
9. smooth
10. modern

Page 70

1. tall
2. angry
3. homely
4. dull
5. boring
6. lake
7. freezing
8. sunny
9. sit
10. whisper

Page 71

1. hurled, tossed
2. carry, lug
3. cold, freezing

Page 72

1. closed, slammed
2. overjoyed, happy
3. furious, mad

Page 73

1. big, gigantic
2. small, tiny
3. speak, whisper